For the young man who faced his night
monsters and demons alone.

Published by Concordia Publishing House
3558 S. Jefferson Avenue, St. Louis, MO 63118-3968
Manufactured in the United States of America

1 2 3 4 5 6 7 8 9 10   05 04 03 02 01 00 99 98 97 96

Hang Your Toes Over the Edge

Robert D. Ingram

Illustrated by Rick Incrocci

Does your bedroom get really scary at night?
When the lights go out, does it cause you a fright?

Do you hear funny noises, like breathing or growling?
Do things watch from the corner, with eyes that are scowling?

Do shadows move? Do they creep closer and closer?
Do toys change, becoming grosser and grosser?

Do you huddle in the center of your bed,
In case something under it has not been fed?

You wouldn't dare hang fingers or toes over that edge.
Who knows what might creep, crawl, or slither under the ledge.

So you pull the covers up over your head,
Holding your breath, lying still, playing dead.

Want to call for help, but afraid to make a noise?
Like to run, but worried those odd shapes are not your toys?

You cannot shout out loud, but you can still pray.
There is One who hears everything you say.

This One is the God who loved you before you were born,
And guards over you through the night and into the morn.

God closes lions' jaws tight, knocks giants out cold,
And defeats iron chariots a thousandfold.

God sees in the darkest dark, and is always close by;
Is stronger than strong, and to save you, would even die.
God's already done it in Jesus, you see;
And God's people are safe, even you and me.

So hang your toes over the edge–God's love protects you!
No monster can ever hurt you. Our God's love is true.

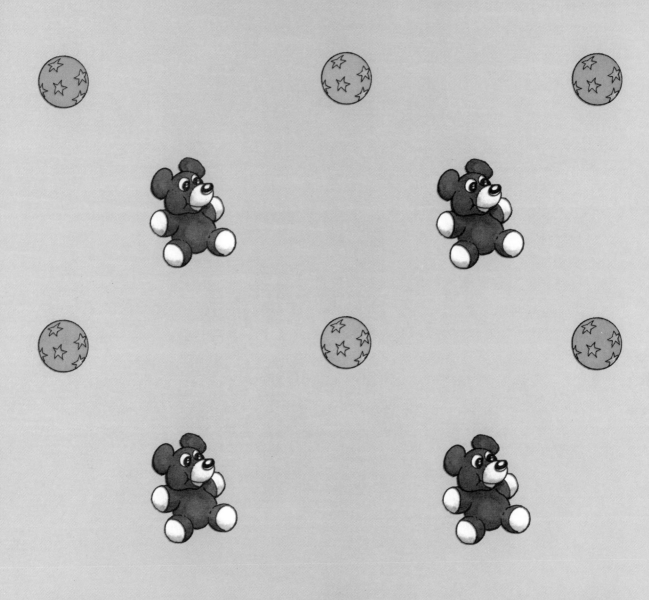